Praise for *Shining Through a Social Storm*

"A unique series for children, by children." -*Booklist*

"At a time when bullying and ahigh in our society, *Shining Through* :lp kids and parents navigate thr(elt appreciation to the authors and on to support kids and parents w we take a stand for both the bull o a higher place that will contribute to a healthy life for a successful life."-Steve Viglione, Founder, CEO of www.iamfoundation.org

"Sorkin tells a moving story that addresses peer pressure, raw emotion, and the power that lies within to survive. I was lured into taking a deep breath as Skylar's characters learned through experiences, viewed situations from different perspectives, and ultimately recognized the impact of their decisions. This story introduces a variety of techniques for building confidence when faced with bullying or teasing situations, and also demonstrates the positive results when a conscious choice is made to stay true to oneself in mind, body, and spirit. Bullying is a serious issue and Skylar conveys a mature and powerful message that it needs to stop. Providing resources and educating our youth to become confident, independent, and respectful citizens begins with stories like *Shining Through a Social Storm*."
-Judy Goldberg, Educator Director, International Learning and Development, Discovery Communications, Inc.

"*Shining Through a Social Storm* is a book that should be shared with all girls 10 and older whether they be part of the 'in crowd' or view themselves as loners or just not fitting in. The book has real-life situations that all girls can identify with and through the resources included in the back of the book solutions that can help every young girl to avoid being a bully or being bullied by others. Bullying is perhaps the most traumatic experience a young person can experience and *Shining Through a Social Storm* reveals that the emotional damage can be just as great as the physical. This is a book that parents should read so they can help identify how they can help no matter what situations their children encounter at school."
-William Gladstone, author of *The Twelve*, co-author of *The Golden Motorcycle Gang*, Founder of Waterside Productions Literary Agency representing best-selling authors Eckhart Tolle, Neale Donald Walsch, and the first *For Dummies* book and authors *of Chicken Soup for the Soul* book series

"This story pulled me right into the world of peer pressure and bullying among girls, yet at the same time models positive, practical ideas to manage these situations. The guidelines that follow have something for everyone...This kind of book is a must-read for parents, kids, school counselors, and anyone helping to support the healthy develop-ment of our youth." -Josh Feder, M.D., Child & Family Psychiatrist, Dir. of Research, The Interdisciplinary Council on Develop. & Learning Disorders

"*Shining Through a Social Storm* is an important contribution to the mental and emotional health for today's youth. It is a brilliant demonstration that creatively portrays the challenges and solutions facing young people as they awaken to their own unique and unlimited potential... Sorkin inspires her peers by providing vital tools to utilize in real-life social storms..." -Angela Amoroso, Exec. Dir. for the Scripps Performing Arts Academy, author of *Surrounded by Angels*

"WOW! What an amazing book written from the heart! Skylar Sorkin's story in the book was a true depiction of the struggles and challenges that pre-teen and teenage girls go through in regards to peer pressure and bullying in their everyday lives. This is an important and beneficial book that is a must-read for all girls!" -Lori Lander, Founder of www.girlsintheknow.org

"*Shining Through a Social Storm* is a must-read for the many parents, teachers and professionals who struggle with finding ways to guide teenagers through the challenging social world of adolescence. The book is filled with practical tips and positive messages that are easy to understand and implement immediately for teenagers and parents trying to navigate through difficult social situations. A toolbox filled with wisdom and hope." -Mara S. Goverman, LCSW, Parent and Child/Adolescent Psychotherapist

"*Shining Through a Social Storm* is a valuable resource for educators and parents when helping young people develop the necessary tools to maintain positive self-esteem. Skylar Sorkin has written an insightful story that I could envision using as a classroom read-aloud during our character trait and bully-proofing instruction." -Debbie Hutchison, M.S., Education, Fullerton School District

"As a parent of three children who will be navigating through these social dilemmas, I particularly liked that *Shining Through a Social Storm* stresses the importance of maintaining healthy friendships and staying true to oneself. The story, and its supporting chapters, written by experts in the field, are a great tool for children and parents alike. It helps us open the channels of communication to assist our children in moving from social pressure into self-empowerment." -Lisa Nelson, Business Owner, Head-Sense.com

"The techniques and practical role-playing scenarios provided in *Shining Through a Social Storm* are invaluable for remembering how to blossom and 'rise above' in the midst of turbulent social waters. This book should be 'the Handbook' that every family refers to again and again..." -Hilary Michels Dunning, Singer-Songwriter, Mother

SHINING THROUGH A SOCIAL STORM

WRITTEN BY
SKYLAR SORKIN
ILLUSTRATED BY SYDNEY GREEN

DEDICATIONS:

To my extraordinary family, whose unconditional love and support help me thrive as a strong, independent girl. I am forever grateful.
—Skylar Sorkin

To my parents for supporting my ideas even when they seem completely crazy.
—Sydney Green

To my beautiful daughter who never ceases to amaze me with your grace, wisdom, compassion, and love. For my son who makes me rethink everything, you are brilliant, dazzling, and kind. You two and your father empower me to gratefully strive to become a better mother, wife, and individual.
I love you all!
—Linda Shook Sorkin, M.A., LMFT

To my aspiring writing students.
—Erica Rood

To Quinn and Teagan, my heroes.
—Adria O'Donnell, Psy.D.

To my boys, Zach and Dylan,
May you always know I love you with all my heart...just because!
—Daniel Friedland, M.D.

To my loving husband and 3 beautiful daughters who support me with my dream to help children to climb over "their rocky mountain" and discover a rainbow of hope on the other side.
—Colleen C. Ster

CHARITY:
A portion of sales from this book will be donated to Isabella's Giraffe Club.

SALES:
The student author and illustrator of this book will be distributing a portion of their earnings into their college savings funds.

4114U: How to Read and Use This Book

Dear Reader,

You may be reading this story for pleasure, or you may have chosen this book because you can relate to its subject matter. Either way, here are some helpful instructions to navigate and guide your way through this book:

1. Read and enjoy the story and notice the vocabulary footnotes; remember the story was written and illustrated by kids just like you. If you have experienced relational aggression, bullying, or some other life-changing event, ask yourself if the characters in this story feel the same emotions you have experienced.

2. After you read the story, you will find a section called 4114U. This section has been put together by experts to give you some helpful tips and advice on how to work through your relational aggression or bullying situation, as well as other significant events in your life. You will find activities to do by yourself along with some helpful activities to do with a parent or loved one.

Because true healing requires you to focus on your emotional, educational, social, and even spiritual needs, we have divided the 4114U portion of the book into the following three sections:

• Action Steps to Help Families Emotionally
• Action Steps to Help Families Socially
• Action Steps to Help Families Psychologically
• Action Steps to Help Families Spiritually

One of our goals is for you to feel like this book was written just for you; we want you to see that many other people struggle with life-altering events just like the one you are experiencing. We also want to give you some hope that things will get better, and to empower you (and your parents) by providing the necessary tools needed to deal with relational aggression.

While we hope you will find this book helpful, please keep in mind that its content is not intended to be a substitute for any professional medical advice, diagnosis, or treatment. We hope you enjoy this book.

All the best,

Colleen C. Ster

President/Publisher, Reflections Publishing

Acknowledgements

A wise elementary principal once told me that our job as parents and educators is to teach our children the coping tools they need. By preparing children for difficult experiences like getting bullied or relational aggression, then hopefully they will have the tips and tools they need in their back pockets to pull out and utilize when necessary.

This is the mission of Reflections Publishing —to allow children to help their peers through the power of their stories and illustrations, and to allow experts to equip kids with the tools needed to thrive in today's world.

This book would not have been possible without the numerous brainstorming and editing sessions with the following people. I thank you for your many hours of dedication and passion to this mission.

Colleen C. Ster
President/Publisher of Reflections Publishing

Educators: Peg Conrad, Julia Hinton, Debbie Hutchison, Janet Orr, and Erica Rood

Business Professionals: Angela Amoroso, Kelley Carlson, Hilary Michels Dunning, William Gladstone, MariJo Gleeson, Judy Goldberg, Lori Lander, Beth Misak, Lisa Nelson, Conchita Ramirez, Steve Viglione, and Tami Walsh

Child Psychologists/Family Therapists: Lynn Dubenko, Ph.D., Josh Feder, M.D., Mara S. Goverman, LCSW, Adria O'Donnell, Psy.D.; Lewis Ribner, Ph.D., Linda Sorkin, M.A., LMFT

Student Editorial Team: Matt Gleeson, Sydney Green, Caroline Ster, Alexandra Ster, and Isabelle Ster

Table of Contents

4114U Section

Published by Reflections Publishing
© 2011, 2012 Reflections Publishing.

This book is a work of fiction. Names, characters, businesses, organizations, places, events, and incidents either are the product of the author's imagination or are used fictitiously. Any resemblance to actual persons, living or dead, events, or locales is entirely coincidental.

First Edition. Published in the United States of America.

ISBN 978-1-61660-004-4

Visit our website at www.reflectionspublishing.com for more information or inquiries.

*   *   *

Other books by Reflections Publishing:
The Real Beauty - ISBN: 978-1-61660-000-6
Written by: Kathryn Mohr
Illustrated by: Kiana Aryan

Face 2 Face - ISBN: 978-1-61660-002-0
Written by: Caroline Ster
Illustrated by: Emily Jones

Scars - ISBN: 978-1-61660-003-7
Written and Illustrated by Parent/Child Team:
Dave, Julian, and Noelle Franco

Foreword

Tami Walsh, M.A.
Founder, Teen Wisdom, Inc.
www.teenwisdom.com

I am very pleased to share my thoughts with you about the special book that you hold in your hands. It contains many of the answers and key insights into the problems and questions I get asked daily in my private practice. As a counselor and life coach for teen girls and their parents, a question I hear on a regular basis is: "How can I make sure my daughter is happy, successful, and well-adjusted?"

During the challenging middle school years, parents repeatedly tell me that they want their daughters to make friends and be accepted by their peers, learn from their mistakes, develop their interests, try their best academically, enjoy their lives, and be able to truly SHINE! And it's no surprise that girls themselves want these same things, too.

However, if there's one topic that challenges these mutual desires, it's the social pressure and difficulties amongst peers that too many girls experience at one time or another during their adolescence. Bullying, "girl drama," and intense meanness are at an all-time high amongst our middle school girls who are experiencing unexpectedly high rates of emotional problems. The National Institute of Mental Health confirms that one in five teenage girls will receive a clinical diagnosis of depression by the time she reaches age 19, and that all other teenage girls are at risk for clinical diagnoses including anxiety, eating disorders, and self-mutilation. Though these diagnoses often have multiple underlying causes, the feelings of social isolation, rejection and persecution by peers are at the core, leaving girls feeling alone, helpless, and desperate. In this technological era where bullying and social aggression do not end when the school bell rings, girls often feel they can't escape the pressure, feel hopeless, and long for genuine connection.

Now is the time to come together: parents, educators, administrators, mental health professionals, and MOST IMPORTANTLY, the girls themselves who desire (and deserve!) to be treated with dignity and respect by their peers, and END the maltreatment of one another once and for all. No longer is it acceptable to believe that "mean behavior" is a "rite of passage" for middle school girls. No longer is it tolerable to have girls come home from school and hide their tear-stained faces in their pillows dreading the next day, and feeling lost and alone. And now, thanks to relatable and important books like *Shining Through a Social Storm,* girls no longer have to do that! Because of courageous girls like Skylar Sorkin, who have used their creative voices to demonstrate the right way girls may choose to interact with one another, girls will now have a chance to actually BE their true selves at school, enjoy a core group of real friends, and be truly happy!

Chapter 1:
Trying to Fit In—It's
a Cruel World!

The morning was gray, damp, and cold. Jayden stepped out onto the balcony outside her bedroom. Breathing deeply, she gazed at the dense morning sky. The misty fog turned everything dreary, including her mood. As she thought about the day ahead, she started to spiral down into an emotional black hole of self-doubt.[1]

[1] self-doubt: to feel that you and your abilities are not good enough

Although she was excited about the upcoming dance audition, it wasn't enough to protect her ill feelings about the peer pressures at school and her obsession[2] with fitting in. No matter how optimistic[3] she tried to be about her dance audition, she just could not stop dwelling on how miserable "The Crew" was making her life. The fear of facing these mean kids for even one more day felt paralyzing.[4] Her self-esteem[5] was fragile and low. She was confused. On one hand, she was a confident, talented dancer who "should" stand strong and have no desire to be part of any group of mean kids. On the other hand, she felt uncontrollably intimidated by "The Crew." She couldn't shake it. So she decided that her only solution was to be accepted by them once and for all.

"Jayden! Sweetie! Your breakfast is ready!" her mom called from downstairs. Jayden closed her balcony door and then paused in front of the full-length mirror to double-check her outfit. An unattractive, ugly twin of herself stared back. She cringed, wondering what people would say about her fashion sense.

---

[2] obsession: to constantly think about something and not be able to get it out of your mind
[3] optimistic: to think positive and be upbeat
[4] paralyzing: to not be able to move
[5] self-esteem: how you feel about yourself and your abilities

Quickly, she threw off her sweats and replaced them with her favorite knee-high socks, jean skirt, and new Abercrombie top. She quickly ran a brush through her long, straight, dark-brown hair, and turned back to look in the mirror. Regrettably, the new outfit failed to change her mood and negative thoughts of herself, and she didn't have time to play her typical round of musical clothes. She had to race downstairs and gobble down her eggs and toast. Grabbing her backpack and jacket, she hurried out to the car. Once again, she wasn't prepared for what the day would bring.

Taking the normal route to school, Jayden's mom started her usual morning check-in with Jayden. "Jayden, you seem a bit off this morning. Are you okay, love?"

Jayden responded with a quick, "Yeah, I'm okay. Just nervous about my dance audition tomorrow." She tried to hide her true feelings from her mom. But her mom knew her all too well. Although their relationship had always been close, and Jayden knew she could rely on her mom for anything, this time Jayden wanted to work through "The Crew" problem herself.

Her mom pulled in front of the school and dropped her off in the carpool lane. As Jayden reluctantly opened the car door, her mom gently touched her arm and said, "Honey, I am here for you when you are ready to talk about what is bothering you." With a wink, she continued, "Now, as far as your auditions[6] go, you will be amazing. Just remember to believe in yourself. Now go have a great day, and I love you tons."

Jayden's parents taught her to love herself despite what others thought of her. However, their valuable lessons seemed to be instantly forgotten when it came to her desire to be accepted by the popular clique.

As Jayden stepped out of the car and onto campus, she lost her grounding when someone yelled, "Hey, nice outfit!" It took all of her courage and energy to walk forward without breaking inside. She knew that familiar voice had come from someone in "The Crew." A tear ran down her face, and she swiped it away. Jayden's mind was flooded with thoughts such as, *I'm so stupid! Why did I wear this? Why can't I stick up for myself? Why can't I just be accepted by "The Crew"?* Confusing thoughts and feelings filled her mind.

[6] auditions: to try out or be judged on your performance

Finally, the bell rang, interrupting her frazzled[7] thinking, and kids scattered in all directions. Jayden sighed heavily, relieved to have class as a distraction.

Jayden's morning classes flew by, and suddenly it was lunchtime. She was surrounded by her closest friends. They sat in their favorite hangout spot, chatting and giggling about the boys they liked…blissfully unaware of the tall girl who was approaching. The blue-eyed blonde strutted into the lunch room, wearing intense, dark eyeliner and designer jeans. It was Brittney, the "queen bee"[8] of "The Crew." Although she despised how Brittney made people feel like they were an inch tall, Jayden couldn't help but want to be in her shoes. Watching Brittney, she started thinking to herself, *Why is she so popular? I have great qualities, and I am a really good person. Brittney is shallow and so evil. Yet, she has everything and I have nothing.*

Brittney walked up to Jayden and her friends confidently, as if she had just won a magazine cover girl contest. "Hey Jay, so I hear you are auditioning for a dance solo? Good luck with that!" Brittney taunted.[9]

[7] frazzled: when someone is out of sorts
[8] queen bee: a person who attempts to control their friends
[9] taunted: to make a remark or joke to make someone upset

Jayden and her friends rolled their eyes in disgust, as Jayden's stomach curled into a little ball of misery. She started to truly doubt herself again, like she always did when it came to Brittney.

"Is something wrong?" asked Brittney, laughing. Jayden breathed heavily in utter frustration.[10] Brittney's immature[11] comments erupted[12] once again. "I can't help that I'm just, like, perfect and you're just a...well, I shouldn't even say it at school!" She turned to walk away, and her hips moved from side to side. Brittney flipped her long, perfect, blonde hair and met up with the rest of "The Crew." Then, out of habit, she started to talk trash about others.

Eventually, the torture of lunch was over, and two class periods later, it was finally time for dismissal.

Laya, Jayden's best friend since kindergarten, came bounding out of seventh-grade English class. She was smartly dressed in her favorite pair of Lucky jeans, a green V-neck T-shirt, and white Vans. Even with her height of 4 feet 11 inches, Laya was spunky and would defiantly[13]

[10] frustration: to be upset when something is out of your control
[11] immature: to behave or think in a way typical of someone younger
[12] erupted: to explode or suddenly break out into laughter
[13] defiantly: to stand up for and refuse to back down

stand up for Jayden—no matter what.

Laya followed Jayden home while explaining all the details of her upcoming birthday party. Confidently she asked, "Okay, so listen, JayJay, who should I invite? Definitely NOT Brittney or anyone else who is part of 'The Crew.' But obviously you, Ciara, Addie, and Carly." She paused in thought, then responded, "I cannot wait!" She did a little jump.

"That sounds great. I can't wait, either!" Jayden tried to sound excited, but she still felt miserable from what had happened at lunch. Suddenly, she burst out, "Oh, sorry, I have to go." Jayden just needed some space and time alone. When she got home, she ran up to her room and sighed in relief that she was finally away from Brittney's hurtful comments. She slowly shut her eyes, and practiced what her dad taught her to do when she was stressed.[14] She began visualizing[15] her worries[16] flowing down a stream far, far away…Letting go, she fell asleep.

[14] stressed: to not be able to relax
[15] visualizing: to form a picture of something in your mind
[16] worries: to be anxious or unhappy about something

Chapter 2:
Stress, Pressure, and the
Miserable Meltdown

The next morning, Jayden woke up tired. She had spent most of the night tossing and turning, thinking about her spring play tryout. She was nervous for the dance audition that would be held during lunchtime later that day.

She had been dancing ever since she was 2 years old, and had always dreamed of achieving a lead part in a school production. Jayden grew up going to these shows to watch various friends and neighbors over the years, and now it was her time to try out for a dance lead at Golden Hill Middle School.

The next morning, Jayden carefully picked out her outfit to wear for the audition. She chose a pair of black, Spandex dance shorts with a long, white T-shirt tied at her waist. She went downstairs to eat a quick breakfast, packed her school bag, and hopped in the car to head to school with her mom. She anxiously rode in the car, trying to contain her feelings from her mom's radar. She could already tell that the day was going to creep along until auditions.

Jayden went from class period to class period until the lunch bell finally rang. Mrs. Lewis, Jayden's school drama teacher, announced on the loud speaker, "Come to tryouts for the spring play! Auditions now in the auditorium. Don't forget your lunch."

Jayden grabbed her lunch and bag, slammed

her locker door, and sprinted to the auditorium. She was convinced that this would be her time to shine; she would even outshine "The Crew."

When she arrived, she found the auditorium to be utterly majestic.[17] It had 300 seats and a sparkling, inspiring[18] stage where real talent could radiate. Although her heart pounded and butterflies fluttered around in her stomach, this was Jayden's only chance to show her talent and prove herself to her peers.

Jayden watched several girls try out for the same dance solos that she was hoping to win. One girl in particular was extremely well-trained and had studied at the local dance studio. Jayden knew that she would be tough to beat.

Mrs. Lewis snapped Jayden out of her daydream by announcing, "Jayden Clark, please come to the stage...play music...and GO!" Jayden's heart opened, and she overcame her self-doubt. Nothing troubled Jayden when she danced. She would lose herself in the music and movement of her body. Her eyes twinkled, and passion[19] ignited her every move. When the music stopped, Mrs. Lewis gave Jayden a huge smile while clapping enthusiastically.

[17] majestic: very big, impressive, beautiful
[18] inspiring: to fill with an urge to do something creative
[19] passion: to have a very strong feeling or belief about something

Jayden knew she had done exactly what her heart and soul told her mind and body to do every step of the way.

Brittney, who was lounging in the auditorium during the audition, was obviously jealous, but she tried to act as cool as possible. While walking to the exit door, Jayden's eyes glanced at Brittney, who glared[20] back with jealousy[21] and disgust.[22] That hateful look almost made Jayden's positive energy pop like a balloon, but she took a couple of deep breaths to recapture the confidence her performance sparked.

Jayden continued walking up the aisle toward the exit, mentally rerunning her performance, step by step, move by move. She walked into a nearby bathroom and stared at herself in the mirror. Her big, deep-brown eyes stared back, and she felt like she had been swept into another world. Jayden continued to mentally replay her audition as if she were watching it on television. Although she was proud of her performance, she was deeply troubled by something altogether different.

Jayden painfully realized that she didn't like how Brittney was able to affect her so deeply,

[20] glared: to look or stare at someone in a mean way
[21] jealousy: to be envious or to want something you don't have
[22] disgust: to be upset or annoyed about something not acceptable

and so quickly. One minute, she was so proud and confident,[23] and the next minute, her confidence was shattered with one look from Brittney. She couldn't grasp how Brittney could have so much power over her. She figured out that she could no longer allow others to walk all over her. Energized by her new realization, Jayden started to engage in healthy self-talk[24]—something her mother taught her to do. Her newfound awareness, combined with her inspirational self-speech worked wonders! She felt lighter, stronger, and self-assured like never before. She triumphantly strolled out of the bathroom to find her friends before class.

All of a sudden, Jayden's ears filled with laughter and she caught sight of the group of kids surrounding Brittney. They seemed to be making fun of Jayden. She questioned herself once again, instantly feeling insecure and confused. Jayden had lost her strength, forgot her positive self-talk, broke down, and cried as she rushed toward the end of the hall to her next class. Jayden sat down at her desk, feeling defeated once again. She glanced up at the clock and convinced herself that she could survive two

[23] confident: the feeling you can achieve again
[24] self-talk: to give yourself a pep talk to work through a situation

more classes, even though she could only focus on getting home soon.

Finally, the day was over. Jayden walked out to the carpool lane and heard the assistant principal yell her name through the bullhorn: "Jayden Clark, your mom is here to pick you up." Slouched over, Jayden walked miserably to the car and explained the whole day to her mom.

"Honey, I am so sorry that you had such a bad day. What can I do to help?"

"Ugh! I hate my life!" snapped Jayden.

"Wow, it was a bad day! It sounds like you need to take some time to gather your thoughts and take care of yourself. Do you want to go for yogurt and talk?" her mom asked.

"Yes, that would be great; I think frozen yogurt and a hug would help."

Jayden's mom always knew what to say and how to help her overcome[25] her problems. She sensed Jayden needed space to find her own solutions. "Jayden, try not to take other people's comments personally. You can't control how others act. All you can do...all you really want to do...is to be yourself. Stand

[25] overcome: to work through an issue and come out on the other side

up for what is right for you. It is not about controlling others, it is about accepting who you are at all times. Also, never, ever forget that your father and I are always here for you."

Her mom's reminders made her feel better in the moment. "Thanks, Mom, I am just worried about what I should do when I am at school and I feel embarrassed or intimidated. Any ideas?"

"I really think you should try to talk to your school counselor when you feel helpless at school or in sticky situations. They are there to support kids in overcoming these kinds of challenges[26]...such as the one you are having with 'The Crew,'" her mom suggested.

"Okay, I will tomorrow," said Jayden, relieved to have finally opened up to her mom. Later that night, after speaking to Jayden's mom in their bedroom, her dad walked downstairs and stared at her with a curious look. "So-o-o-o, how was your day at school?" he asked.

"It was, like...horrible! 'The Crew' are just a bunch of bullies, and like..."

Compassionately, her dad said, "Talk slower, Jayden. I can't understand you, and you are saying 'like' way too much."

[26] challenges: something that tests your strength and abilities

"Stop interrupting, Dad! Okay? I'm so stressed, and I…" Knowing her dad meant well, and being the overprotective type he has always been, Jayden felt loved, but misunderstood and frustrated that he would try teaching her a lesson at such a wrong time.

Suddenly, letting go of all her emotions, she sobbed,"I had a bad day, Dad, and I don't feel like being judged like I am at school!" She ran upstairs and took as many deep breaths as possible, trying to calm herself down. Her heart raced; she thought it might explode and break into little pieces.

When her tears stopped flowing and her head stopped spinning, she began to relive the memories captured in the pictures of her friends on her bedroom wall. Jayden's heart once again sang as she embraced[27] the love and good times she shared with her true friends.

Feeling more composed,[28] Jayden started to walk back downstairs. She thought about what her mom had told her regarding the difference between true friends and "frenemies."[29] Her understanding of the situation became much more clear. As she moved through her house,

[27] embraced: to eagerly accept
[28] composed: state of feeling calm
[29] frenemies: an enemy disguised and a person who is not a true friend

her eyes scanned the surroundings, soaking in every little detail. Her home and the things in it gave her a sense of comfort and safety. Her negative thinking melted away.

She found her parents sitting in the living room and apologized for her rude tone and for storming upstairs. "I just feel so much stress from school, and when I come home, I just want to escape from all the drama and pain."

Jayden's parents understood how distraught[30] she had become, and how she needed time to regain her composure.

With a loving tone, they said, "We are glad you feel better, but we still think it would benefit you greatly to meet with the school counselor tomorrow. That is, if you feel you need the support."

Jayden agreed to schedule a meeting with the counselor, although she wasn't fully convinced it would help.

---

[30] distraught: so upset that you can't think clearly

Chapter 3:
Are They Really That Cool?

On the way to school the next day, Jayden's mom reminded her to speak to the counselor if she felt it would help. "Jayden, it is okay to reach out for help. School counselors and teachers are there for you when we can't be. They are also trained for this exact kind of thing," she said.

Jayden turned away from her mom and rolled her eyes. "I know, I know," she mumbled. She was worried what others would think or say if they found out. Jayden thought kids who went to talk to the school counselor were labeled[31] as rejects, weak, or insecure freaks.

When they arrived at school, Jayden got out of the car and walked toward the school gates. She still kept hearing her mom's voice in her head, encouraging her to see the counselor, but she was also deeply worried that Brittney would find out.

She could visualize[32] the look on Brittney's face and imagine hearing the teasing[33] in her head: *Jayden, you're such a weak little baby. Telling on me to the big bad counselor...really? Did you go sit and cry on your mommy's and daddy's laps, too?* Jayden was so lost in thought that she barely noticed Brittney walking up to her.

Brittney looked as gorgeous as ever on the outside, smiling and appearing to be a messenger of good news. Jayden was really confused. Brittney had never approached her in a kind and friendly manner.

"Hey Jayden!" Brittney said with kindness instead of taunting. "I just wanted to tell you that you did awesome at the auditions. I was wondering if you might want to hang out with, and, well, actually be a part of 'The Crew'?"

Extremely puzzled, Jayden waited for a

[31] labeled: to be named or identified in a certain category
[32] visualize: to picture in your mind
[33] teasing: to make fun of someone or be cruel

"Just kidding!" or something much worse, but it never came. Jayden started thinking, and her mind flooded with the possibilities: *Has it finally come? Am I really being asked to be a part of "The Crew"? Brittney is so powerful and cool. Did my audition finally prove I was "cool" enough to become one of the most popular girls at the school? No more pressure. Why am I even hesitating? I should just go for it. Just say yes! Pain no more!*

"Yes!" Jayden blurted out impulsively. She was so taken by her excitement that she forgot about the endless bad Brittney memories. With a one-track mind and not thinking about what her surprising response might mean to her closest friends, Jayden headed toward her first class with Brittney. Her original plan to meet with the school counselor was now a distant thought from the past.

In class, Brittney started passing notes to Jayden. Jayden asked herself, *Should I pass notes? I could get in serious trouble! If I don't do it, Brittney could get mad and kick me out of "The Crew"! I just got in! What should I do? Oh whatever...* She looked down at the paper and started reading Brittney's note.

> Hey girl~
>
> Oh my gosh, I heard that Brian is going out with Jessica. They are such a gross couple.
>
> Eee-w-w-w.
>
> He is way too cute for her!
>
> ~B

Jayden grabbed her pencil, and wrote the meanest words she had ever written to another person:

> B~
>
> I know...He is too cute for her!
>
> ~J

Brittney grabbed the note from Jayden and

stared back in approval of Jayden's partnership in crime. The bell rang and the teacher announced, "Okay kids, pack up—time to go."

The first three periods passed, and Jayden had no idea of the drama that was lying ahead of her. Jayden met Brittney and "The Crew" at the quad. While walking toward them, Jayden felt very nervous; her palms were sweating as she wondered if "The Crew" would actually like her.

"Hey, JayJay!" Brittney called. "Okay, so these are all of our friends." Brittney introduced each member: "First, meet Izzie, who is my closest confidant and 'go-to friend.' We all respect and follow her advice." Izzie, with her sporty, short haircut and freckles, smiled out of the corner of her mouth.

"Next, meet Mike. He looks tough with his dark, thick, muscled build and buzz haircut, but he is really just a teddy bear. He does everything I tell him to do. I mean EVERYTHING." Mike shrugged his shoulders as if he didn't care.

"Now this is Jordan. Don't let his spiky hair fool you. I call him my fan because he is like a groupie that follows me around." Jordan grinned in agreement.

"Moving on to Emma…we all love her, but she doesn't have a thought of her own. She spends most of her time getting the boys' attention by wearing short shorts and flipping her long, luscious, blonde hair at them. She pulls in many victims whom we all eventually devour." The girls exchanged a devilish look.

"This is Kayla, we love her…and her money. She funds our group and stirs up loads of drama. She is also our fashion queen. I get two outfits and a pair of shoes every month with her daddy's credit card!" Brittney struck pose in her designer outfit.

"Now, meet Justin—the basketball champ. He is the most loved boy in school! I really use him for popularity and to make all the girls jealous. Basically, he's the school's athletic Justin Bieber." Brittney blew him a kiss.

"Last, but not least, is Zac. We pretty much only tolerate him so we have someone to cheer for at the football games." Zac shrugged and rolled his eyes.

Jayden greeted each "Crew" member with a nervous smile. She faintly remembered what her mom taught her about kids in cliques: There is typically one "queen bee" and many random followers. Brittney continued, "Well, since you are officially part of 'The Crew,' you have to fit in with us so that we don't look like idiots with any stupid behaviors or bad fashion sense. So, say 'hi!' to your new 'Crew' and go tell your old 'Crew' 'goodbye.' Ready? Set? Go!" Brittney commanded, as she pushed Jayden from the back. Reality hit Jayden hard as she realized she wasn't made to act this way. She was stuck on the spot. She was being told to leave her true friends for the popular kids.

In shock from both excitement and the dread of carrying out Brittney's command, Jayden said, "Although I'm thrilled to be friends with you and be part of 'The Crew,' I still want to keep my other friends. They're really great, especially when you get to know them. Maybe it's possible we can all hang out sometime?"

"Well, do you want to be in 'The Crew' or not?" Brittney asked. "You have to choose, because frankly, your 'old' friends are losers!"

Jayden was torn, but ultimately she refused to give up the idea of finally having power and becoming popular. So Jayden caved, deciding to ditch her friends for a chance to be seen as cool. With false confidence, Jayden cautiously[34] and awkwardly approached her old best buds to carry out Brittney's final demands.

She just couldn't believe what she was about to do, and felt as though she were outside of her body. Shamefully, Jayden slowly tapped Ciara's shoulder. In a distressed[35] voice, she said, "Hey girls, I'm sorry, but I have been invited to be part of 'The Crew' now. So I guess it's time for me to move on...um...," while rolling her eyes to the sky, and with a big nervous gulp..."I'll see ya around." Jayden couldn't grasp what just happened. She heard the words come out of her mouth, but she didn't feel like she was the one who said them.

Jayden's best friends looked at her as if she was joking. They chuckled at first, before realizing that she was serious.

Jayden remained shocked by the words she had just said to her longtime childhood friends.

Their faces turned surprised, worried, and then sad beyond words. Laya, in particular, was speechless. She just stared at Jayden with shock, sadness, then anger. Laya, who knew how sensitive Jayden was, fired back, "Well, do

[34] cautiously: to be careful and leery
[35] distressed: painful or upset

you really think Brittney will be loyal? What will happen when she no longer has a need for you? What will you do then, Jay?"

Jayden pretended to ignore her comment, but it really struck a chord. Laya had always been a "24/7 friend"[36] to her. As Jayden turned and walked away, Laya's jaw dropped open in disbelief.

When she got back to "The Crew," Jayden paused, trying to absorb what she had just done. She couldn't believe she had just ruined her childhood friendships. Jayden's heart broke. She felt sick.

Then Brittney appeared. "Are you okay, Jay?" she asked.

"Yeah... I think so."

They began walking down the hall together. On the inside, Jayden felt rotten and evil, but she didn't change her mind. There was a part of her that was overtaken by the power of popularity and hanging out with Brittney.

As the week went on, Jayden found herself trying to act more like Brittney. She started participating in bullylike behavior, spreading rumors,[37] backstabbing,[38] gossiping,[39] and more than anything, not being herself.

[36] 24/7 friend: true friend 24 hours a day, 7 days a week
[37] rumors: information passed on about someone that may or may not be true
[38] backstabbing: to talk about someone behind their back
[39] gossipping: to spread truthful or untruthful words about somebody

By the end of the week, Jayden couldn't stand to continue pretending anymore. She couldn't tolerate feeling lousy and trying to act like someone else, especially not someone as mean as Brittney. She realized she had no option.

Jayden desperately wanted to talk to Laya. She saw Laya standing by her locker. When Laya saw Jayden, she rolled her eyes and quickly turned her back. Jayden felt even worse. She felt like she was stuck in the body of a bully and felt controlled by the "queen bee" Brittney.

The following day, Jayden woke up and was hit by a clear understanding that she needed to get back to her real self and real friends—the person she was before she joined "The Crew." The solution was to redeem herself once and for all.

Chapter 4:
Victorious

The week was finally over, and Jayden was glad to have the weekend to regroup. She was totally exhausted from the prior week and couldn't concentrate on much else except getting out of her mess. Her mind kept wandering back to why she had even gone down this path of trying to become popular. For as long as she could remember, she had wanted to be a part of "The Crew." She badly wanted Brittney to accept her. But now she knew Brittney only truly loved herself. Brittney was all about power and control. She wanted to be the center of attention because that was all she had to define herself. Jayden thought she needed power and attention to feel happy, but realized she had so much more to draw on in life. She had great, loyal friends. They may not be the most popular group in school, but they were honest, kind, and real. Jayden also had a love and talent for dance. Her ability to perform entertained others and brought her joy, confidence, and passion. More than anything, she recognized how badly she missed her friends.

Jayden grabbed an old photo album off the shelf to remind herself of who she was and who her genuine friends were in her life. This reminder motivated and focused her on what had to happen on Monday. She flipped to the first page of the album and started gazing at the pictures. There they were—Laya, Ciara, Addie, Carly, and herself—smiling, laughing, and having the best time ever. She wished she could rewind and start all over, but she started fearing it was seriously too late. Her thoughts were then interrupted by the sound of her parents' footsteps.

"Honey, can we talk? Did you ever meet with the school counselor this past week?" Jayden's mom asked.

With all the drama, Jayden had completely sidestepped the counselor. She thought about lying to her parents, but she just couldn't. She was done with acting like she was someone else for one day.

"Oh, Mom and Dad. I'm so sorry. I totally didn't. I did the opposite."

"What do you mean you did the opposite?" her mom asked.

"I just can't talk about it right now," said Jayden.

Still fishing to find out what was going on, her mom said, "Dad and I want to help, but we also want you to learn to ask for help, so things don't get out of control at school. The last thing we want is for our advice to make you more frustrated."

With that, they left her alone. Jayden's attention returned to the photos for comfort and hope. She never wanted to betray her friends. They meant more to her than Brittney and "The Crew." She couldn't believe how poor her decision-making was when it came to being a part of the "in" crowd. Her true friends never pressured her to gossip, backstab, or spread any rumors. They just always had a blast together.

That night, Jayden still couldn't sleep. She couldn't escape the nightmare she had created. She tossed and turned as her mind kept spinning uncontrollably. She couldn't wait to straighten things out.

Jayden started thinking in steps. First, she vowed[40] to be honest with everyone, including herself. Second, she rehearsed what she would say when she saw her friends and "The Crew" that upcoming day.

Initially, she would walk up to "The Crew" and tell them what was honestly on her mind. Then, she would genuinely apologize to her friends and ask for another chance. Third, she vowed to never act out in a negative manner to anyone, even Brittney or other members of "The Crew." Jayden knew it would be hard to fess up, but she was willing to do whatever it took to prove herself and make up with her friends. With a clear plan locked in her heart, she fell asleep.

[40] vowed: to make a promise

Chapter 5:
A Taste of Karma

The next morning, Jayden jumped out of bed, full of energy she didn't expect to have. She was ready to face both her real friends and "The Crew." Plus, the spring play cast list was going to be posted. She quickly got dressed and looked herself over in the mirror. Instead of focusing on any negative thoughts about her appearance, she focused on the strong, beautiful girl staring back. Then she bounced down the stairs to the kitchen.

"Hi, Mom!" Jayden said, beaming.

"Wow, Jayden, you sure seem happy this morning. What's going on?"

"Mom, I've made a decision."

"A decision about what, honey?"

"Well, at the beginning of the year, I felt like 'The Crew' was the most amazing group ever! But you helped me realize that being popular doesn't define me."

Jayden's mom had been listening intently. "Okay, tell me more?" she asked.

"I wanted so badly to be friends with them, especially Brittney. I felt honored when she invited me to hang out with her group, but then the drama started. They insisted that in order to be a member of 'The Crew,' I would need to gossip about almost everyone in school, hang out with just them, and get rid of my best friends! When I finally met all of 'The Crew,' I realized they weren't that interesting and they are definitely NOT cool. In fact, I have nothing in common with them. Now I deeply fear that I have forever ruined my friendships with Ciara, Addie, Laya, and Carly."

With sincere concern, her mom replied, "Sounds like you made some poor decisions this week and now you are facing the consequences. So how did all of this happen? And besides, weren't you going to talk to the counselor if you had trouble?"

Jayden began to tell her mom everything that happened. "Well, I was actually on my way to the counselor when Brittney suddenly surprised me with the invitation to actually be in 'The Crew.' I was so blown away, Mom! I immediately felt like ALL of my problems were solved, and my future was brighter than ever. It didn't take much time to realize that I was badly mistaken! My problems got much worse in a deep and heart-crushing way. I learned that being 'in' is actually being 'out.' I realized that being popular can sometimes be negative, especially when such power is used to control and hurt others. I was surrounded by negative popularity this week, and it made me feel horrible. I ended up acting like them, just to fit in. That's not who I am and NEVER someone I want to become. I have a lot of repair work to do, and I'm ready to do it. I have a plan."

Jayden's mom listened intently with genuine amazement that her daughter remembered all of their long talks and the lessons she tried to pass on to her. Although she was surprised that Jayden could flip-flop so quickly on her childhood group of friends, she was confident her daughter was on the right path. While proudly nodding, she said, "Okay, great! So, what's the plan?"

"Today, I'm going to confront 'The Crew' and tell them that I can't be a part of any group that treats people so poorly. It is not worth it just to be seen as 'cool.' Then I'm going to face my friends with my heart in hand, asking for another chance and a commitment to prove my sincerity."

Her mom smiled and said, "That is a very mature thing to do! You're really standing up for what's right, Jay, and I am proud of you for realizing that your '24/7 friends' aren't worth trading for the 'so-called' popular kids. As you know, your dad and I are here to help, but we know you can do it!"

Jayden arrived at school early, feeling empowered[41] but a little nervous. She raced to Mrs. Lewis' room to see the cast list that had been posted. Rapidly scrolling down the list, Jayden found her name next to the part of dance soloist and did a little jump with two claps.

Jayden moved on to the next item on her agenda. *Okay, now off to initiate the plan,* she thought. She never had to stand up to such a popular and powerful group before, but there is a first time for everything.

She saw Brittney off in the distance, waving for her to come over. The butterflies in her stomach madly started fluttering, but she remembered what she saw in the mirror: a confident girl, ready to be herself.

"Hi, Jayden! You look cute. Love the shoes! By the way, I hear Laya is having a birthday party and no one wants to go!"

Courageously[42] and faithfully[43] sticking to her plan, Jayden responded, "Brittney, you don't have the right to say that about Laya. She's my dear friend. She would never talk about me like that or treat anybody else that way." She

---

[41] empowered: to give someone control over their own situation

[42] courageously: bravely

[43] faithfully: to be loyal to something

swallowed hard and continued, "Brittney, what I like about you is that you have something deep inside of you that makes you beautiful and strong. After getting to know you better this past week, I finally understand what makes you special is NOT how you treat people. Underneath your mean attitude, there is probably a kind and honest part of you that is hiding behind your desire for power and control. Maybe if you tried to be nice, it would feel good and even more people would want to be with you."

Brittney was mortified. "What did you say?" she squeaked out, embarrassed that "The Crew" heard every word.

"I said that I want to be your friend, BUT NOT if being your friend means being hurtful to other people. I don't want to be a part of any group that gossips, backstabs, or spreads rumors. It is not worth it just to be popular," Jayden said.

Brittney was dumbfounded.[44] No one had ever stood up to her. She couldn't think of a good comeback, so she did the only thing she knew to do. She stomped off, demanding that the other members of "The Crew" follow her.

---

[44] dumbfounded: in shock and disbelief

However, much to her surprise no one moved. Brittney quickly turned and shouted with fear, frustration, and confusion: "Whatever! I have better things to do, and you will all be sorry!"

Everyone stood in awe, especially Jayden. She felt proud and relieved. Then Izzie, another member of "The Crew," turned to her and said, "Wow, I have never seen someone stand up to her like that. I have felt trapped by Brittney for years and never said anything to stand up for myself. Pretty impressive! I didn't know you had it in you, Jayden. Maybe we can still hang out sometime?"

"Sure thing," Jayden said with a wink.

Thank goodness that's over. Now I need to find my true friends, Jayden thought. She walked toward the spot she used to hang out with her old buddies. Jayden saw them turn their backs as she drew near.

Jayden cleared her throat, mustered her courage, and said, "Hey there...I would be extremely upset if any of you did what I did. I know I was totally wrong and beg of you, for just one minute, to hear me out...can you give me a minute, please?" None of the girls turned their heads. Jayden didn't expect this to be easy, but she thought they would at least talk to her. She continued, "I know I was more than a mean bully. I was pressured and gave in when I had a chance to be popular. I thought 'The Crew' would accept all of you once I became friends with them. I hoped it would be different, but I realized I lost my true self and my true friends. I made the worst decision of my whole entire life. I need you guys and hope for another chance. I need a chance to prove my loyalty and make up for my behavior. I promise you that I'll never do it again."

None of her old friends spoke.

Laya finally broke the silence. "You really hurt our feelings, Jayden, and now we don't know where we stand. You totally abandoned us for her …the 'mean girl.'"

Jayden sighed deeply. "I know, if I could take it back right now, I would—I swear! But unfortunately, I can't. I am sorry and, largely because of this, I told Brittney and 'The Crew' that I am no longer part of their group. I hope that's a good start to prove myself to all of you. I will do anything to go back to the way things were."

Laya, Ciara, Addie, and Carly turned toward Jayden cautiously. "Do you really mean what you're saying? Do you promise that you will never turn your back on us again?" asked Laya.

"Yes, I really, really mean what I am saying. I promise I will never betray you again. I love you guys!"

The girls felt Jayden's sincerity, and because they understood, they forgave her. They hugged and—soon enough—giggled, just like old times. "We're so glad to be friends again, Jayden. Now we know that you're back to your real self," declared Ciara.

"We love you!" said Laya.

* * *

Jayden grabbed the lipstick, getting ready for the performance. While finishing her makeup, she heard the door open.

"Honey, are you so pumped up or what?" questioned her mother.

"Yeah, Mom. I really am. I'm just going to do my best. Showing the world what I have is a gift, and I don't care what Brittney or anyone else thinks or says. Not everyone is going to like me!" Jayden said confidently, realizing the words she spoke were true to her core.

"Well, I am so proud of you, love. You have learned and grown so much from this tough experience. Now it's time to apply what you've learned on this stage, right here, right now!"

"I can't wait! Thanks for your support. You're the best! Love ya!" exclaimed Jayden.

"Break a leg, honey!" Jayden's mom said as she walked out of the changing room.

Jayden squeezed her hands together while visualizing herself doing the best she could ever do. Then she heard a beep in the dressing room, and she knew it was time to shine. Jayden took off her jacket, fixed her hair, and took three deep breaths, knowing in her heart and soul that she would be amazing! She strutted out in her gorgeous costume, jumping up and down and getting herself pumped up. Jayden had no false image to play and no fitting in to do… just being herself and performing was all that was needed. Jayden got into her position onstage and started dancing like there was no tomorrow. After she landed her last leap, she finished with a triple pirouette.[45] With her eyes twinkling and soul shimmering, she proved again to herself that she was born to dance. The music stopped, her heart swelled with gratitude, and Jayden cried with joy.

Jayden's dance was the perfect ending to the show. Thunderous claps erupted from the audience and they gave a standing ovation for Jayden and the entire production. Jayden smiled, and looked around until she found her friends and family in the crowd. The one person who wasn't clapping was obviously Brittney, but this didn't affect her. If anything, Jayden felt compassion toward Brittney because she knew why she wasn't clapping. Jayden soaked up the good energy. To her surprise, the greatest joy was not because people were giving a standing ovation, it was the fact that she had just focused on being herself and letting things unfold the way they were supposed to go. She was free from worrying about others, and empowered by no longer needing approval to feel good about herself.

At the post-performance dinner with her

---

[45] pirouette: a ballet move to turn in place on one leg

parents that night, Jayden shed tears of joy and understanding. She said, "I can be anything I want to be. I learned my lesson and realized that being popular is not what it's cut out to be. I found my way back to my authentic[46] self. I discovered that I am so grateful to be who I am…both the good and what needs improvement. I am so lucky to have connected with the amazing power of my mind, heart, and soul. My life is not about seeking approval or fitting in anywhere. It's about being the best me I can be. It's focusing on the relationships that make everyone involved better because of it. It's about being loving, caring, and kind and not letting people take advantage of you. Most importantly, I learned that the only way to realize my dreams is to live my life inside out! Gosh, life is a trip! I love you guys!"

The waiter walked up to the table, as Jayden wiped her tears of joy, and said, "Your garlic fries are almost done." Jayden looked at her dad, knowing that he was equally as excited…her next challenge was already on! Getting enough fries before her dad gobbled them all down.

[46] authentic: original

4114U
(Information For You!)

Written by:
Linda Shook Sorkin, M.A., LMFT - Family Therapist
Erica Rood, M.A. - sixth Grade Teacher
Adria O'Donnell, Psy.D. - Child Psychologist
Daniel Friedland, M.D. - Medical Scholar

 Our intent is that you will read through this 4114U section with your parent or guardian. Please read and discuss the tips and tools provided as you process this information together. Our goals are for you to create a game plan that will help you navigate through stressful situations of relational aggression, and identify your true group of friends through your own self-empowerment.

 A parent's job is to give their children the tools needed to navigate, and to be active participants in solving problems that will invariably come their way in life. Relational aggression can be very unsettling for children, and by reviewing the following pages together, you can develop a game plan of action.

Hopefully, this book will open up a wonderful world of communication where together, you and your child can safely navigate through tough situations and sail to an enhanced life.

Action Steps to Help Families Emotionally

Written by:
Linda Shook Sorkin, M.A., LMFT
Teen & Family Specialist
www.soulempoweredcoaching.com

Social Aggression on Emotional and Psychological Well-Being: It's an Inside Job

- "One out of every four kids will be abused by another youth."
- "...77% of students are bullied mentally, verbally, and physically...14% of those who were bullied said they experienced severe reactions to the abuse."
- "One out of five kids admit to being a bully or doing some bullying."
- A research study shows that kids who have been bullied or bullies themselves are at a higher risk of experiencing: "loneliness, trouble making friends, lack of success in school, and involvement in problem behaviors such as smoking and drinking."
- Playground statistics revealed that every seven minutes a child is bullied on the playground with adult intervention at 4%, peer intervention at 11% and **no intervention at a whopping 85%.**

- Recent statistics from the American Justice Department

Relational aggression (expressed against others as bullying, peer pressure, gossiping and/or identity crisis, self-doubt, anger, and neurosis) directly impacts the quality of life and development of a child into adulthood.

Relational aggression can affect a child's path into adulthood filled with resentment, addiction, stress, and broken relationships—an overall bitter outlook on life. Strangely enough, it doesn't matter much whether the child is giving or receiving the social aggression; they each produce similar results.

Social experiences directly impact our children's self-esteem and their ability to perform, as well as to make decisions and choose friends. The National Self-Esteem Association (NSEA) provides a definition of self-esteem that any parent wants for their children:

> Individuals who accept responsibility for their actions, have integrity, take pride in their accomplishments, who are self-motivated, willing to take risks, capable of handling criticism, loving and lovable, seek the challenge and stimulation of worthwhile and demanding goals, and take command and control of their lives. They trust their own being to be life-affirming, constructive, responsible and trustworthy.

NSEA also claims:

> Self-esteem is strongly connected to a sense of competence and worthiness and the relationship between the two as one lives life. A sense of competence is having the conviction that one is generally capable of producing desired results, having confidence in the efficacy of our mind and our ability to think, as well as to make appropriate choices and decisions. Self-esteem stems from the experience of living consciously and might be viewed as a person's overall judgment of himself or herself pertaining to self-competence and self-worth based on reality.

Just like Jayden battled through her "Social Storm," we need to support our children with self-esteem building methods to help them navigate through relational aggression. As parents, we need to help them trust, rely upon, and relate to others in all social environments from a place of internal grounding.

Social aggression cannot harm the child who refuses to be a victim. It also cannot harm the child who understands that social aggression is not a reflection of the child's identity and that it is mutually exclusive from their core of self-acknowledged worthiness.

This book is about self-empowerment and personal strength. It's about embracing relational aggression as a means to strengthen character development, and generate self-esteem that opens doors to a spectacular future for our children. This book is intended to help make your child's dreams more than possible—doable! Before we get into the tools, let's take a quick look at today's world and the unique challenges that we, as parents, need to understand and confront.

Today, relational aggression is radically different because of the advancement of modern technology. Social media not only makes bullying a pervasive, easy, and unrelenting tactic for kids to target others; it also serves as a power platform, dousing our kids with inappropriate information, unrealistic benchmarks, impossible expectations, and mixed messages from what we try to teach our kids at home.

Technology gives inside access to the "aggressors" who intentionally harm others. A child's reputation, and even identity, can be altered in a matter of one click: one posting, e-mail or text.

Kids can no longer leave school and escape the face-to-face wrath of mean kids. Self-identity takes on a whole new meaning in today's world. A child's life can be severely altered while being home safe, asleep in bed. Cyberbullying via social networking sites such as Facebook, Twitter, or blogging can spin stories about any kid, whether the story is based on facts or not. The resulting impact from such published slander, in either case, degrades (or threatens) a child's self-esteem, identity, trust, and their ability to adjust in life.

Every time the computer is turned on, the trauma continues. It is incredibly difficult for children to escape the wickedness of social drama, and recuperate, without fearing what will be said or done through social media channels.

Even younger children are not immune to the torment of "social ladder" climbing; they, too, can suffer in silence while navigating through the terrain of elementary school. Unfortunately, social drama today begins at a much younger age than you would expect. Unprecedented access to television and computers expose our children to undesirable behaviors before they even enter kindergarten.

It has been reported that students as young as second grade struggle with incidents of bullying and relational aggression. The need to fit in, belong, and feel accepted ranks high even among the youngest.

On a positive note, more media attention and programs have begun to emerge within schools to create "bully-free" environments. But, even with these community events in place, the most powerful and immediate solution is at home with attentive parents.

As parents, we have a great responsibility and power to influence and mold our child's reality. We need to equip our children with self-reliant skills to help them grow—even in the face of inevitable social aggression. Acquiring this skill set will make them better citizens and highly competent individuals. As a result, children will learn to operate from a place of higher self-esteem, compassion, and well-being as they venture off into adulthood to shape society for future generations.

Game Plan: What to Do?

Awareness is the first step to creating change. Understanding the dynamics of your child's social world is vital in staying in tune with their development. Keeping a check on the pulse of their social world will allow parents to prevent the fallout from social drama. If parents and other adults inspire children to be their best selves and learn the coping skills to navigate through their social worlds, they will be better equipped to handle difficult situations and succeed more in life.

Barbara Coloroso, author of *The Bully, The Bullied, and the Bystander*, believes there are three roles involved in the cycle of bullying. She reveals, "The bully, the bullied, and the bystander are three characters in a tragic play performed daily in our homes, schools, playgrounds, and streets." This play is a present-day reality and the ramifications can be life-threatening, as we have witnessed in the media.

Inevitably, you can be sure your child has or will play one of these characters at some point in their lives. Therefore, it is our duty, as parents, to empower them with social skills, and to realize each of these "characters" need to take responsibility for their actions in order to make a change in the cycle of bullying.

Symptoms Checker

What to look for if you suspect your child is a: target, aggressor, or witness

Target

Sad, tearful, angry outbursts, withdrawn or isolated, trouble in school, change in friends, loss of interest in regular activities, and/or changes in appetite. If you notice any of these signs and/or your child isn't openly communicating, it is time to investigate.

Aggressor

Be in tune with your child's social world. Watch for any behavior changes and communication feedback from teachers and friends. It is also important to note that sometimes a "bully" can be as good as gold at home, but a holy tyrant at school.

Witness

Children involved in a bystander role can feel helpless in knowing what to do. They may be fearful that the "aggressor" will retaliate and they will become the next "target." As a result, sometimes the "witness" will take a passive role and won't speak up for what they believe is right. Other times, they don't have the guts to be the main "aggressor" who instigates offenses, but are able to get some power needs met by aligning with the "bully." Regardless, "witnesses" should know that if they do not stand up for the "target," then they could be labeled as guilty as the perpetrator. Often times, if an "aggressor" knows their bad behavior will get reported and consequences enforced, they will stop.

Bottom Line

Keep your eyes open to any behavior changes in your child. Address them immediately.

Parents: # Tips for Parents of a Target

#1 **Ask direct, open-ended questions:** Have heart-to-heart conversations with your children. Talk with them openly and ask them questions that will elicit a deeper response than a simple "yes" or "no." You are attempting to gather as much information from them as possible, which also enriches your relationship with them in the process.

#2 **Listen to them!** Make sure you are listening to your child with a compassionate and empathetic ear. They need to know you are there for them and can come to you when needed. Don't make judgments about their situation. Don't ignore or downplay their feelings or experience.

#3 **Coach your children** on how to stand up for themselves, solve problems, set boundaries, handle stress and conflict, and have a voice. Ultimately, teach them not to be a target. Show them how to deflect someone else's insecurities.

#4 **Practice role-playing** with your child to ingrain preemptive confidence in their abilities to handle difficult social and relational situations.

#5 **Reflect their true nature.** See the good in them. Teach them independence and to love and honor themselves. Focus on character development and how to successfully handle stress and conflict. Educate your child about social group skills with their friends and discuss how to belong and fit in appropriately. By teaching in this context, you will be addressing your child's innermost needs and innate rights to freedom and well-being in their skin. Ideally, this is done through leadership by example.

#6 **Educate them** on how not to personalize an "aggressor's" actions. It is very important to provide insight into the "aggressor's" behavior. They need to see that the aggression has nothing to do with them personally, but more to do with the "aggressor's" own low self-esteem and/or experiences in their own life. In other words, there is a deeper reason for an "aggressor's" bad behavior—**and it's not your child.**

#7 **Encourage** compassion toward the "aggressor." Explain to your child that the "mean" individual is usually trying to fulfill an unmet need. This will not only support your child in discerning a deeper reason for bad behavior, but also help them to develop the skill of compassion. Having compassion for those who wrong us is one of the most powerful psychological and emotional "tricks in the book." It's not easy to do, but it pays off in the end.

#8 **Get your kids involved** in activities that they can excel in and feel personally competent, and empowered.

#9 **Invite other children over** for play dates or hanging out. Help them to find friends who are supportive and bring out their best qualities.

#10 **Monitor** Internet and cell phone texts. Sites such as http://www.safetyweb.com and http://www.socialshield.com may be helpful. Also, keep in touch with other parents.

#11 **Provide a safe environment** at home. Do not tolerate bullying or intentional aggression between siblings at home. This will simply show acceptance of that behavior. Also, it helps to make your home a peaceful environment for your family to rejuvenate after "slaying dragons" in their daily life.

#12 **Love them up!** Let your kids know you've "got their back" at all times.

Parents: Tips for Parents of an Aggressor or Witness

#1 **Investigate any accusations** that your child is bullying others. Don't automatically defend your child without understanding the perspectives of all parties involved. Otherwise you will miss out on a valuable teaching moment for your child.

#2 **Help them to understand** the meaning behind their behavior. Find out what areas in their life they are struggling with and get them support.

#3 **Reinforce character development,** your family values, and morals.

#4 **Help them with problem-solving** and conflict resolution.

#5 **Teach them compassion** and empathy for others. These are crucial skills for kids to learn in order to connect to a deeper and more meaningful level with others.

#6 **Choose effective consequences** for your child's "bullying" or aggressive behavior.

#7 **Insist on making amends** with the "target." This is one of the most important experiences for them to learn. It will teach self-responsibility, remorsefulness, and integrity. Don't pass up on this lesson! This can be done verbally or in a written letter. Face-to-face amends are usually the most effective. They need to face up to their wrongdoings.

#8 **Encourage the "witness"** to have a voice and speak up if they observe relational aggression.

#9 **Explore motives with the "witness."** What are they avoiding from not speaking up? Look into any fears they may be experiencing and teach assertiveness skills.

#10 **Role-play** appropriate ways to treat others.

#11 **Review** the previous tip list and put some suggestions into action as well.

It is imperative for parents with an "aggressor" to understand and communicate the long-lasting personal consequences of aggressive behavior. Children must understand the detrimental effects their behavior can have on their own future, too. **Be very clear on what successful behavioral change looks like, and how an "aggressor" or "witness" can be part of the solution.** Finally, reiterate the payoff that changing behavior from social aggression or negligence to social support and relational harmony can do. Point out role models who exhibit mutual respect, kindness, tolerance, and an appreciation for difference.

Action Steps for Children

First and foremost, it can be difficult growing up in today's world, having to find your place, and fitting into a "specific" group of friends.

As you come across different types of people, be open and be aware of your judgments. Just because someone acts, looks, or smells different from you doesn't mean they are strange and/or weird...just different. We would have an incredibly boring world if people were all the same. So, stay open, curious, and learn from what you encounter.

Likewise, even with an appreciation for differences among your peers, there is MEAN behavior everywhere you go. As a result, it is important to understand that people are mean for several reasons —and these are reasons that factually have NOTHING to do with who you are!

- Desperately need to fit in and be cool
- Desire attention from others
- Want to feel superior
- Feel inadequate, insecure, or powerless
- Crave power or control
- Depressed, angry, miserable state of mind
- Disconnected from family members or family problems
- Intolerant, ignorant, sense of entitlement, or isolated
- Jealous or manipulative

Can you see how all of the above examples have literally nothing to do with you? Instead, they have everything to do with the person who is being hurtful and aggressive. It is the "mean" person's inability to get their needs met and deal with their own life effectively that is at the core of their behavior.

Learning to navigate through your social world is crucial. Your self-esteem can be altered if you continually find yourself in situations where you lose your power and feel inadequate. Knowing how to handle yourself in social settings, drama, or conflict, while always staying true to yourself, will help you thrive in life. Knowing that the behavior of others usually has nothing to do with you is a critical foundational understanding you must embrace.

Kids Tips for Children

#1 **Don't ever take another person's behavior personally!** Author Alan Cohen so eloquently states, "When someone is unkind or abusive toward you, don't take it personally. Anger is more about the giver than the recipient. If you accept their attack as a statement about you, you will not see clearly, and the situation will be even more muddied. Do not accept their 'gift,' and you will help them face their own issues."

#2 **Speak up** and have a voice if you feel threatened or see any acts of bullying or relational aggression. Always talk to a parent, teacher, or authority figure.

#3 **Journal your feelings** and express your thoughts and concerns.

#4 **Talk to your parents** to share similar experiences they had growing up.

#5 **Hang with friends who bring out your "best" self.** A good friend is someone who inspires you to be a better person, not one who tears you apart.

#6 Find ways to **empower your friends.** The more you give, the more you will receive.

#7 **Practice compassion** for others. It helps to see an "aggressor" as someone who doesn't know how to treat others with respect for one reason or another. It's in YOUR best interest to forgive and practice compassion for those who have wronged you.

#8 **Don't react** when you are bullied, put down, made fun of, ignored, or excluded. Instead, respond calmly, walk away, surround yourself with supportive friends, or ask for help. If an "aggressor" sees that they are getting to you, this will only fuel the fire. Sometimes they prey on the "weak" or look for opportunities to raise their social status.

#9 If you are the "aggressor," **honestly look within** yourself and uncover what motivates you to be cruel to others. This takes a lot of courage, but if you come clean and find alternative ways to manage your social and emotional world, you will become a better person. Hurting others is NEVER the way to get ahead in life! You are only hurting yourself...what comes around goes around!

#10 If you are a **"witness," speak up!** Either stand up to the "aggressor," support the "target," or anonymously ask for help. Being passive can fuel the aggressor by misplacing the power. Many times, the "witness" fears that they will be the next one to be attacked. Fear is an emotion that can be paralyzing and all-consuming. Remind yourself that your fear isn't always reality. Talk with your parents or guardians to get guidance.

Kids & Parents: Final Thoughts

It takes a village to end the cycle of bullying and relational aggression. Parents, teachers, administrators, and kids themselves are all needed in making a lasting positive change. Most importantly, as parents, be aware of your child's social-emotional-psychological life. Be involved, support, guide, empower, and love your kids. Be respectfully inquisitive and assess their viewpoints, monitor whether their perspectives sound empowered or deflated. Take the temperature on their emotions. If you continue to see signs of depression, stress, or unusual levels of distractibility, be careful and assert yourself supportively. Find a way to make sure they know that they're NOT ALONE.

Children need you and look to you as a model for proper, effective, and compassionate behavior toward themselves and others. As Gandhi said, **"Be the change you want to see!"** Be the parent, friend, spouse, and individual who you ultimately want your child to be.

In conclusion, the path of higher self-esteem is the path of the self-empowered child. Parents are the best source and resource for fostering inner strength. Teachers and coaches are the next influence in line to facilitate self-reliance and courage to stay above the negative influences.

Convince your child of their innate internal strength and you've done the best job a parent can do.

Action Steps to Help Families Socially

Written by: Erica Rood, M.A., Sixth Grade Teacher

It's not uncommon to hear parents or teachers say that a little teasing here and there is a part of growing up. In reality, however, these taunts and teases can be extremely damaging to a child's sense of self and their academic success. In many cases, teasing can turn into intentional harm or bullying. As parents and teachers, it is important to be aware of the various types of bullying and how they can manifest for both boys and girls. Bullying occurs when a person is psychologically or physically maltreated by another person on an ongoing basis. Sometimes, it's not easy to identify bullying because it may happen out of an adult's sight, or because victims won't show their feelings or tell someone right away. It is helpful for adults to become familiar with the five types of aggressive behavior, which are considered by experts to be bullying behaviors. They are:

- Covert aggression
- Physical or overt aggression
- Verbal aggression
- Reactive aggression
- Proactive aggression

- **Covert aggression,** which is indirect and typically takes place within the social groups of girls. It includes social isolation and the exclusion of others.

- **Physical or overt aggression,** which is more likely to occur between boys. It is direct and involves intentional acts of violence. These actions can be physical or verbal and include threats to another's well-being.

- **Verbal aggression,** which includes spoken threats, put-downs, and name-calling.

- **Reactive aggression,** which occurs when non-aggressors turn into aggressors in an attempt to defend themselves.

- **Proactive aggression,** which includes intentional behaviors whose purposes are to accomplish a goal. This may include excluding someone to maintain social status.

While both boys and girls are equally likely to experience bullying at some point in their lives, the way in which they respond to bullying differs. When placed in a combative situation, boys will either "fight" or "flee" the situation. Boys tend to express their anger in a physical way and then move forward. Girls, on the other hand, have a different reaction to the stress caused by these types of situations. Instead of expressing their feelings or leaving the situation, girls search for support from their surrounding environments.

Game Plan: What to Do?

Parents: Action Steps for Parents

First, learn and talk about the problems caused by bullying. For example, victims of bullying can have an extremely hard time forming and maintaining intimate relationships with peers because they may avoid social situations or experience social anxiety. Victims tend to feel lonely and rejected, which makes paying attention in school very hard. It's not at all unusual to see a victim's grades drop, or to exhibit acute emotional responses, such as anger and sadness. In extreme cases, victims feel so desperate that they contemplate or even commit suicide. Educate yourself and your family about these devastating effects so they can begin to understand how words and actions impact others.

Second, keep track of bullying behavior. If your child is complaining about being bullied, ask for details and write down specific dates, behaviors, and reactions. It is important to know when and where bullying occurs, as well as how peers and other adults are reacting. Maintaining records is essential to a successful intervention.

Third, if you think a child is a victim or perpetrator of bullying, get involved! Interventions should include parents, teachers, community, and students. Parents can benefit from learning strategies on how to manage aggressive children and support victims of aggression. There are a great many resources available online and in the bookstore. Along the same line, children also need strategies for identifying and responding to aggression.

Kids Action Steps for Children

Learn and practice what to say, how to hold yourself, and what tone of voice to use in the face of a bully. Role-play different scenarios with friends or other adults so you are prepared when/if you are ever faced with a bully. Talk to your parents, teachers, or other responsible adults. Reflect on the following questions or use them in a conversation with your friends:

1. How much of your conversations with others revolve around gossip?

2. What do you want and need in a friendship?

3. What are your rights in a friendship?

4. On what grounds would you end a friendship?

5. What are your rights and responsibilities as a friend?

One of the most important things you can do to overcome difficult experiences with friends is to create, maintain, and communicate your personal boundaries. Be clear what your boundaries are in a friendship. Be true to yourself and honest with your friends.

Action Steps for Teachers

"Let's Work Through It" Activity
Directions: Use to teach strategies
for pro-social behavior.

#1 Start by asking individuals to anonymously write down a description of a "sticky situation."

This is a social experience that posed or would pose a problem. It can be something that has actually happened or something they think would be hard to resolve. Some ideas include: what to do when someone calls you a bad name, or what to do when a group of friends doesn't include you in a game or other activity.

#2 After writing the situation, form groups of three to four individuals.

#3 Pass out one card to each group to brainstorm various ways the problems could be handled and what solution is best and why.

#4 Ask groups to prepare a dramatization of the problem and the various ways it could be solved—both healthy and unhealthy. Engage in a discussion about the many ways to solve a tough problem. Point out the healthy, pro-social approaches to social problem solving and encourage the use of those approaches.

Kids & Parents: Final Thoughts

Teachers and parents have the power to affect the ways in which children relate to one another. First and foremost, they are models. The way adults interact with one another shows children how to act with one another. When talking to students or to your own child, take time to ask questions and listen to their answers, opinions, and thoughts. Try to steer them away from allowing themselves to be misguided by initial assumptions. Adults owe it to themselves and their children to be involved. Talking with your child about friendships and bullying is the first step. Then, encourage them to talk with their friends and practice strategies they can use if/when they are faced with a tough situation. Be open and honest; be a role model and teacher; be a listener and an advocate for the well-being of all children.

Action Steps to Help Families Psychologically

Written by: Adria O'Donnell, Psy.D.
Comic Drawings by: Garrett Richie, age 12

We all start conversations with the best of intentions—especially with our children. Parents desire open communication with their children, but are quickly confused and frustrated when seemingly simple discussions go awry. The following comic strips highlight how parents can use specific talking points to better communicate with their children.

Simply adjusting the questions you use to start the conversation, or listening more than you talk, may cause significant shifts in the quality of your conversations. Many children and adults may not be aware of the stress they have accumulated throughout the day. When you ask, "How was school today?" your child may honestly not know the answer, hence the response "Fine." Additionally, you may not understand why they have a seemingly random meltdown later that night about having to wash their hair (even though they KNOW it is a "hair-washing night") or whatever the trigger may be.

Talking Points for Parents

Parents:

#1 **Ask open-ended questions.** Asking the right questions will get you the right answers. "How was your math test?" may result in a one-word answer, such as "Fine." Instead, try, "Tell me what kinds of problems ended up on your math quiz?" If you get "IDK" (I don't know), try again.

#2 **Pick your timing.** Just because YOU want to talk about something does not mean that your child does. If you start to strike out, meaning your child shuts down…back OFF! Revisit the conversation later. A child who feels pressured to talk won't feel relaxed enough to be honest.

#3 **Don't ask them how their day was.** "How was your day?" is a bad question. Instead try, "Tell me two things that happened today that were really funny." Note that this is not a question, but a request. Create conversation starters such as "Hey, make me smarter—tell me one thing that you learned today that I might not already know."

These talking points should yield more of a dialogue. When you get a one-word answer, you have probably asked the wrong question.

Respond vs. React. There is an enormous difference between these two things. When children share about their day, about who said what to whom, we parents have an emotional response. We get upset if someone has teased them, or disappointed when they get in trouble with teachers. **Responding** means that we say what we feel or think regarding what the child has shared, showing empathy. For example: "You know, it is not okay for her to talk to you like that. You must have felt really sad." **Reacting** is quite different. For example: "She called you a WHAT? That little brat. You shouldn't play with her any more." Reacting is rawer and has more of your emotions, which can overshadow your child's emotions. If a child has to manage your feelings, they will not process their own. This is easier said than done, so practice saying things more softly, leaving room for his or her feelings.

SHUT UP and listen! Your child wi'' want to talk when you do NOT. They ' get chatty in the bath, when you are t them into bed, in the car, or cle dinner dishes. During these time' "window is open," stop talking You do not have to have any answers at the time of disc rushing into your advice: "' you should do...?" Just li' restating what you heard ι me get this straight, you v best friend Sue who said, 'Yo to eat with us today'...is

#6 **Be present during transition times.**
If you have the luxury of taking your kids to or from school, watch to see who runs to greet them, or who runs away. Scan to see what is going on and who is involved. Body language, posture, and facial expressions can tell you a lot about how your child is feeling as they start and end their day. During these moments, observe your child's "group entry skills." How a child joins in play is a very significant social skill.

If you sense that your child lacks this social skill, you must help them to scan the setting before they ask to play. Literally stand back with them, looking at peers' faces and listening to their words.

Ask questions about what they see and hear, and role-play with them about how to enter the game. Some kids ask to play too quietly or too loudly. Some children ask to play, but then take over the fantasy, which may irritate their peers. Some kids simply don't "get it" and quickly become the brunt of the game.

Topic: Learning Group Entry

A Compliment Goes a Long Way

Topic: Asking the Right Questions

"Bad Question" Take 1

Topic: Asking the Right Questions

"Good Question" Take 2

Topic: Opening the Floodgates

Blah...Blah...Blah Take 1

Topic: Opening the Floodgates

Shut Up and Listen! Take 2

Topic: Brave Talk Coaching

Pushing Your Agenda Take 1

Topic: Brave Talk Coaching

Shut Up and Listen! Take 2

Action Steps to Help Families Spiritually

Written by: Daniel Friedland, M.D.
Founder and CEO, SuperSmartHealth
www.supersmarthealth.com

What is more painful than being rejected and abandoned by others? Rejecting or abandoning ourselves. It's painful enough to suffer the judgment, criticism, rejection, and abuse of others in bullying. Even more painful is when hurtful comments and behaviors become internalized; soon people turn toward self-judgment or self-criticism, which leads to overwhelming feelings of self-doubt and ultimately self-abandonment.

Self-doubt, or even more specifically doubts of self-worth, is very threatening to our psychological well-being.

In a study personally conducted on self-doubt at the airlines' gates of San Francisco International Airport in 2000 (previously unpublished data), more than 300 people between the ages of 13 and 76 were surveyed.

Three questions were included to determine just why self-doubt is so threatening to us:

1) Did you feel that you received more love and acceptance growing up when you succeeded than when you failed?

2) Do you tend to accept yourself more when you succeed than when you fail?

3) How bothered are you by feelings of self-doubt?

A statistician then analyzed the results. The following correlations were found to be highly statistically significant.

Participants who most strongly agreed with Question #1 agreed most strongly with Question #2 and tend to accept themselves more when they succeed than when they fail. These individuals also reported being most bothered by doubts of self-worth.

The conclusion from this part of the study is that we are conditioned to fear self-doubt. Our childhood conditioning results in a subconscious contract that becomes embedded as a circuit of implicit memory in our brains. It states, "I will love and accept myself if I prove self-worth."

The corollary to this contract is, "If I discover I am not worthy, I cannot accept myself."

This is what makes bullying and the ensuing feelings of self-doubt ultimately so threatening. When the bully judges, criticizes, or rejects us, what's most threatening is not that they invalidate us, but that we internalize their invalidation and believe that we are indeed unworthy, and as a consequence of our contract, we fear that we might abandon or invalidate ourselves.

In response to this threat of self-doubt, we instinctively fight or take flight. We fight to prove self-worth by trying harder to fit in, or we take flight from anything that triggers self-doubt such as avoiding any conflict or standing up to the aggressor. For some, this threat can be so intense that they may take the ultimate flight. Deeply shamed by their aggressor, they may tragically seek the physical death in suicide to escape the more painful alternative of living invalidation, or living death.

An awareness of this childhood contract is liberating. It offers an empowering solution for parents and children seeking resilience around feelings of self-doubt, and an inoculation from the effects of bullying that plagues our society.

Game Plan: What to Do?

Parents: **Action Steps for Parents**

First, parents can empathize and normalize their children's feelings of self-doubt. You can let your children know that when others judge, criticize, or reject them, it's natural to experience doubts of self-worth, and that you have experienced this, too.

Next, express your unconditional love for them. Let them know they are lovable, even when they doubt they are worthy; it's when they need this the most, even if they are absorbed in their pain and seem emotionally unavailable to receive your love.

Unconditional love is more than a healing balm. When expressed consistently, it cultivates a healthy version of the childhood contract and builds resilience.

In the Self-Doubt Study, participants who stated that their parents loved them as much when they failed as when they succeeded, valued themselves equally, too, and were least bothered by feelings of self-doubt.

Essentially, their contract reads, "I accept myself, doubts of self-worth and all."

Thus, an aggressor may hurt them, but with an enduring sense of unconditional love, they are more able to stand firm and take care of themselves in these painful moments.

Giving unconditional love to our children is easier said than done. It's hard not to celebrate and feel proud when our children do well, but let our disappointment bleed out when they don't. So practice mindfully to express your love for them when they might least expect it. Surprise them!

Knowing that I can do better with expressing unconditional love for my two boys, I like to play a little game with them.

I ask them the question, "Do you know why I love you?" They answer, "Why Dad?" and I respond, "Just because."

Then, I have a secret handshake with them whenever I say goodbye or goodnight. It involves a bunch of knuckle-slapping, but always ends with us hugging heart to heart. In these moments, I feel they know they are loved and that this is hopefully hard-wiring unconditional self-acceptance—doubts of self- worth and all—into their developing and impressionable brains.

Game Plan: What to Do?

Kids — Action Steps for Children

If much of our underlying suffering as adults stems from our unconscious childhood contract stating, "I will love and accept myself if I prove self-worth," then children have a wonderful opportunity. The ink with which they have written theirs is not yet fully dry and can more easily be rewritten.

Here is a contract that can be used:

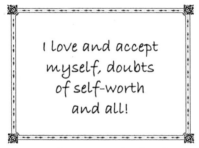

I love and accept myself, doubts of self-worth and all!

Or, better yet, if you can think of another version of this contract that more fully expresses your own unconditional self-acceptance, write it here and paste it in a place where it's visible to you each day.

How then can children begin to embed this contract? The key lies in how children treat themselves in the moment when self-doubt arises, like when it's triggered in bullying. It's important to not only provide our children support, but also to encourage them to treat themselves with the same care and compassion they would a give close friend going through similar circumstances.

In the midst of suffering from self-doubt, seeking inner guidance can also be immensely helpful. Research has shown that a sense of connection with something larger than oneself can facilitate healing and decrease suffering. In Dr. Harold Koenig's book, *The Healing Power of Faith*, his research indicates that when people are faced with health problems or life challenges, it is the individuals with strong belief systems have the best overall, positive recovery. When people can believe in something bigger than themselves, they can often heal faster and experience less pain.

From a scientific perspective, whatever we ruminate on shapes our brain. Our thoughts create neural circuits that strengthen their connections and become embedded as neural destiny. So, if we ruminate on questions such as "Am I worthy?" self-doubt becomes more embedded in our brain. On the other hand, if we seek inner guidance with questions such as, "How can I better take care of myself?" or "How can I find strength in something larger than myself?" these circuits of self-care, faith, and resilience strengthen, too.

The following is a practice designed to help you care for yourself and find inner strength and resilience in your challenging situation. The more you practice these steps, the stronger these related brain circuits will become.

You can do these steps all by yourself, or have someone you care about such as a parent or trusted counselor read them to you as you do them. If it helps, you can also make a recording of these steps and play this recording back to yourself as you do them.

#1 Stop and notice the thoughts, emotions, and sensations in your body.

Name your thoughts, emotions, and physical feelings. (Example: "Judging myself." "Here's sadness." "Tightness in my chest.")

#2 Know you are not your thoughts, emotions, and sensations, but that these are just little bursts of activity that move through your brain like clouds moving across the sky.

#3 Now shift your attention to think about a time you felt most loved, or think of someone or something that you love.

#4 Notice where you experience this feeling of love in your body.

#5 Now, as you breathe in, imagine you are breathing in through this place where you are feeling love in your body, and that your breath is being enriched by this love.

#6 As you breathe out, imagine that you are filling up your entire body with love.

#7 Then, when you feel a greater sense of calm, seek inner guidance by asking inspiring questions in your thoughts such as, "What else can I do to take care of myself?" "Who can I turn to for nourishing support?" "How can I best express myself in this situation?"

#8 Continue your breathing and pay attention to any answers that may come to you.

If the answers feel right and are good for you and others, then ask for the courage and support to take any action that would be helpful to you in this challenging moment.

Continue breathing love in and throughout your body, asking inspiring questions and paying attention to any answers you may receive for a few minutes or as long or short as you feel is helpful to you. If your mind drifts back to painful thoughts, recognize this and come back to your loving breath.

Experiment and modify this practice as is most helpful to you. Make this process your own. Explore ways of simplifying. For example, if you find it helpful to just focus on the steps of breathing love in and throughout your body alone in the middle of feeling stress, go with this. If you find it helpful to focus more on seeking inner guidance by thinking of inspiring questions to ask, then practice this.

As you practice, know that you are worthy of love and acceptance no matter what your thoughts, emotions, and experiences are. Notice and appreciate how you are taking care of yourself as you are doing so. Draw strength from this.

Donald Hebb, who is considered by many to be the father of neuropsychology, is most famous for his contribution to neuroscience when he stated, "Neurons that fire together, wire together."

Activating self-compassion in the midst of self-doubt binds these two brain circuits of experience together. Essentially, you are hard-wiring the contract, "I love and accept myself, doubts of self-worth and all."

By seizing the opportunity to take care of yourself when you are being bullied, those who bully you only help to make you stronger. In these moments of practicing self-compassion, you triumph over those who bully you. You take back your power.

While dealing with relationship aggression is immensely challenging, transforming your pain with this practice of self-care will help you to grow more resilient. You will become more confident and powerful knowing you are worthy and able to love and accept yourself no matter what!

About Our Experts:

• Adria O'Donnell, Psy.D.
www.drodonnell.com

Dr. Adria O'Donnell is a licensed clinical psychologist practicing in San Diego. Since 2001, she has specialized in working with children and adolescents, with a specialization in teen girls. Her foci are on social skills training for adolescents, learning disabilities, tech-aggression, and relational aggression, a more covert form of bullying often used by girls.

In these areas, Dr. O'Donnell has become a coveted public speaker and has developed several pioneering programs. She helped create the "Girls ROCK" program for the Junior League of Pasadena and two programs for grammar ("Brave Talk") and middle and high school-aged kids ("Straight Talk"), which teaches conflict resolution skills and assertiveness training.

Dr. O'Donnell speaks locally about the effects of technology on teens' social and emotional development. Her lively workshops bring the timely, latent issues of psychological aggression and victimization in middle school-age girls to the fore.

Dr. O'Donnell earned her Bachelor's Degree at the University of San Diego in Communication and Hispanic Studies, attended the University of Granada, Spain, and earned her Doctorate from the California School of Professional Psychology, San Diego.

• Linda Sorkin, M.A., LMFT
Founder, Soul Empowered Coaching
www.soulempoweredcoaching.com

Linda works with tweens, teens, parents, couples, and families as a licensed therapist, certified teen life coach, and specialist in self-empowerment and relationships. In addition to her private practice, she consults and develops content for companies and community-based programs to support parents, faculty and kids. Linda offers a unique hybrid approach, "Therapeutic Coaching," that combines various aspects of traditional therapy with proven and unique coaching strategies through which years of her private practice and real-life experiences get applied. Linda is also a certified yoga instructor, where she combines her passion for self-awareness and yoga to create programs, train, and support individuals to enhance their lives physically, emotionally, and spiritually. Linda has a B.A. in Communications/Psychology/English from UC Santa Barbara and an M.A. in Clinical Psychology from Pepperdine University.

· Daniel Friedland, M.D.

Founder and CEO, SuperSmartHealth
www.supersmarthealth.com

Daniel Friedland, M.D., is a thought leader, keynote speaker, educator, and consultant in Evidence-Based Medicine and Health and Wellness. He is board certified in Internal Medicine and is the author of *Evidence-Based Medicine: A Framework for Clinical Practice*, one of the first textbooks to guide physicians on this widely utilized approach to making effective medical decisions. Inspired by his medical training at the University of California, San Francisco (where he is currently an Assistant Clinical Professor of Medicine), he discovered how the framework of evidence-based medicine not only promotes scientific intelligence, but also cultivates emotional intelligence to achieve a more holistic experience of health and well-being. An in-demand expert in decision-making and promoting scientific and emotional intelligence, Dr. Friedland has delivered programs to physicians, allied health care professionals, patients, the U.S. Army, Air Force and Navy, executives and employees in Fortune 500 companies, and for Vistage, a leading global network of CEOs. Dr. Friedland serves as Medical Director for Barney & Barney insurance brokerage, on the Board of Directors for the American Board of Integrative Holistic Medicine, and as the Founder and CEO of SuperSmartHealth, which provides seminars, consulting, health coaching, and wellness programs, including the 4 in 4 Framework™ to achieve peak performance. This program empowers you to navigate stress, uncertainty, and self-doubt and optimize your health, relationships, and productivity.

· Erica Rood, M.A.

Del Mar Union School District
Sixth Grade Teacher

Miss Erica Rood has been teaching in the Del Mar Union School District for seven years. During this time, she taught both fourth and sixth grade. Prior to that, she taught in London and spent five years at Del Mar Hills Nursery School, teaching pre-kindergarten and kindergarten. Miss Rood has her B.A. in Liberal Studies, with a minor in Child Development. She has a Multiple Subject Teaching Credential and a Master's in Education. Her Master's thesis focused on relational aggression and intervention strategies for sixth-grade students. Recently, she earned an Administrative Credential, but her love for teaching has kept her in the classroom. In her free time, Miss Rood enjoys reading, traveling, staying active, and enjoying her beautiful hometown of San Diego.

Web Links:

- Bully Safe USA
  http://www.bullysafeusa.com
- Committee for Children
  http://www.cfchildren.org
- Cohen, Alan - Author
  http://www.alancohen.com
- Common Sense Media's free Digital Literacy and Citizenship Curriculum
  http://www.commonsensemedia.org/educators
- Crick, Nicki - Researcher
  http://www.cehd.umn.edu/icd/SocialDevelopment/Default.html
- Kidscape - Preventing Bullying, Protecting Children
  http://www.kidscape.org.uk/
- Ophelia Project
  http://www.opheliaproject.org
- Rigby, Ken - Researcher
  http://www.kenrigby.net
- The Coalition for Children
  http://www.safechild.org
- SafeTeens.com: Internet Safety for Teens
  http://www.safeteens.com
- SocialShield.com
  http://www.socialshield.com
- Stop Bullying Now! U.S. Department of Health & Human Services
  http://www.stopbullying.gov/

References for Adults:

- Coloroso, Barbara. *The Bully, the Bullied and the Bystander: From Preschool to High School – How Parents and Teachers Can Help Break the Cycle of Violence.* New York: Harper Collins, 2003.

- Dellasega, Cheryl and Charisse Nixon, Ph.D. *Girl Wars: 12 Strategies That Will End Female Bullying.* New York: Simon and Schuster, 2003.

- Farber, Adele and Elaine Mazlish. *How to Talk So Kids Will Listen & Listen So Kids Will Talk.* New York: Harper Collins, 1980.

- Fried, SuEllen and Dr. Paula Fried. *Bullies, Targets & Witnesses: Helping Children Break the Pain Chain.* Lanham, MD: Rowman & Littlefield Education, 2009.

- Koenig, Harold G., M.D. *The Healing Power of Faith: Science Explores Medicine's Last Great Frontier.* New York: Simon & Schuster, 1999.

- Kupkovits, Jamie. *Relational Aggression in Girls: A Prevention and Intervention Curriculum with Activities & Lessons for Small Groups and Classrooms.* South Carolina: Youthlight, 1999.

- Olweus, Dan. *Bullying at School: What We Know and What We Can Do.* Malden: Wiley-Blackwell, 1993.

- Senn, Diane. *Bullying in the Girl's World.* South Carolina: YouthLight, Inc., 2008.

- Simmons, Rachel. *The Curse of the Good Girl: Raising Authentic Girls with Courage and Confidence.* New York: Penguin, 2009.

- Simmons, Rachel. *Odd Girl Out: The Hidden Culture of Aggression in Girls.* New York: Harcourt, Inc., 2002.

- Wiseman, Rosalind. *Queen Bees & Wannabes: Helping Your Daughter Survive Cliques, Gossip, Boyfriends, and the New Realities of Girl World.* California: Three Rivers Press, 2009.

References for Kids (Grade Level):

- Cristaldi, Kathryn. *Samantha the Snob.* New York: Knopf Doubleday Publishing Group, 1994. (K-2)

- Kaufman, Gershen, Lev Raphael, & Pamela Espeland. *Stick Up for Yourself: Every Kid's Guide to Personal Power & Positive Self-Esteem.* Minnesota: Free Spirit Press, 1999. (5-12)

- Ludwig, T. *Just Kidding.* Berkeley: Tricycle Press, 2006. (2-6)

- Ludwig, Trudy. *My Secret Bully.* Berkeley: Tricycle Press, 2005. (4-6)

- Ludwig, Trudy. *Trouble Talk.* Berkeley: Tricycle Press, 2008. (1-4)

- Madonna. *The English Roses.* New York: Callaway Editions, 2003. (4-8)

- Moss, Peggy. *Say Something.* ME: Tilbury House Publishing, 2004. (2-6)

- Munson, Derek and Tara Calahan King. *Enemy Pie.* Canada: Raincoast Books, 2000. (K-3)

- O'Neill, Alexis. *The Recess Queen.* New York: Scholastic, 2002. (1-3)

- Penn, Audrey. *Chester Raccoon and the Big Bad Bully.* Terre Haute, IN: Tanglewood Press, 2008. (2-5)

- Romain, Trevor. *Cliques, Phonies, & Other Baloney.* Minnesota: Free Spirit Press, 1998. (3-8)

- Sachar, Louis. *Holes.* New York: Farrar, Straus, and Giroux, 2008. (6-8)

- Sachar, Louis. *Sixth Grade Secrets.* New York: Scholastic, 1992. (4-7)

- Simmons, Rachel. *Odd Girl Speaks Out: Girls Write About Bullies, Cliques, Popularity, and Jealousy.* Florida: Harcourt, 2004. (6-12)

- Spinelli, Jerry. *Stargirl.* New York: Random House, 2000. (6-12)

- Sprague, Susan. *Coping with Cliques.* California: New Harbinger Publications, 2008. (6-12)

In-Depth 4114U Concepts:

Book Club Discussion Questions:

Written by Erica Rood, M.A.

1. Discuss Brittney's character. In the beginning, Jayden thinks because Brittney is pretty and popular, she must be happy. Is this an accurate assumption? Why or why not?

2. What if Brittney had used a social media such as Facebook as a tool for teasing Jayden? Discuss how social media can be used for both positive and negative interactions with friends. How can you protect yourself from what others post? How should you respond to a negative post?

3. Despite her fear of being teased, Jayden goes through with the auditions and has an awesome performance. Since she was doing something she loved, it was easy for her to shine. What are some things that fill you up with positive feelings? How can you create more positive experiences in your life?

4. In the beginning of the story, Jayden doubts herself and listens to her negative thoughts. What are some ways you can overcome self-doubt and stop yourself from listening to the negative voice in your head?

5. What are some things you love about yourself? Make a list of qualities you are really proud of and frequently remind yourself of those qualities.

6. After Jayden tells her BFFs that she is no longer friends with them, she is filled with regret and realizes they mean more to her than "The Crew." She makes amends by apologizing and promising never to betray them again. Have you had to make amends with a friend after doing or saying something you regret? Share some ways to make amends.

7. Brittney pressures Jayden to gossip and backstab. Discuss the role peer pressure plays in friendships or social groups. Share some ways you can deal with peer pressure and avoid doing things that you don't want to do.

8. When Jayden makes a decision to stand up for herself, she suddenly feels positive and strong. Discuss how your thoughts can affect your actions and your view of yourself.

9. At the end of the story, references are made to a "true self." Can you outline qualities of your true self?

10. There is a strong theme of trust in the story. Discuss the role trust plays in a friendship. Discuss what it means to trust yourself and why that is important.

11. Name some reasons why groups include and exclude people. Are there any good reasons to exclude a person?

12. When Jayden stands up to Brittney, Izzie thanks her and says "she has been trapped by Brittney for years." Discuss reasons why a person might feel trapped in a friendship or group. What are some ways to resolve that feeling?

13. Discuss the importance of popularity. What makes certain people popular? Share positives and negatives of popularity.

14. At the end, Jayden has a powerful realization. "The Crew" essentially become popular by putting other people down. Read the below quote and discuss reasons why you should never give your power or control to another person.

> I learned that being 'in' is actually being 'out.' I realized that being popular can sometimes be negative, especially when such power is used to control and hurt others. I was surrounded by negative popularity this week, and it made me feel horrible. I ended up acting like them, just to fit in.

15. Jayden talks to herself a lot in the story. Sometimes, she tells herself she's stupid for wearing something or for being too scared to stick up for herself. She also talks herself into standing up to "The Crew." This is called self-talk. Discuss ways you can create more positive self-talk.

16. In Chapter One, Jayden was not happy with how she looked and felt scared that "The Crew" would tease her for what she was wearing. Discuss the difference between how you look on the outside and how you feel on the inside. Is what you look like always a true reflection of who you are? Why do girls care so much about how they look?

17. Why do you think Brittney changed her attitude toward Jayden and asked her to join "The Crew" after the auditions? What does this tell you about Brittney's character?

18. Discuss ways to deal with a person like Brittney or a group like "The Crew." What role do you play in your group of friends?

CPSIA information can be obtained at www.ICGtesting.com
Printed in the USA
LVOW102139110312

272611LV00009B/26/P